EXTREME ANIMALS

DEADLIEST!

20 DANGEROUS ANIMALS

STEVE JENKINS

HOUGHTON MIFFLIN HARCOURT · BOSTON · NEW YORK

Deadliest!

Contents

Danger!

For millions of years, animals have been killing and eating other animals. And over that time, both predators* and prey have developed some amazing ways of hunting or defending themselves.

Animals use teeth, claws, poison— even electricity—to get a meal or escape danger. And a few creatures, such as sharks and crocodiles, sometimes see humans as food. Luckily, most animals don't want to eat us. But if we are not careful, many of them can still be deadly.

* Words in blue can be found in the glossary on page 38.

Hunters use fangs, venom, and other deadly weapons to catch and kill their prey.

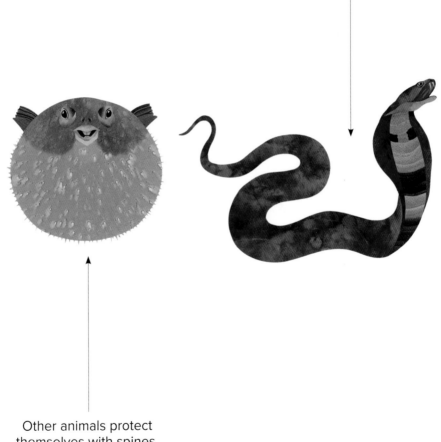

Other animals protect themselves with spines, poison, or a powerful kick.

Bull sharks will swallow almost anything. Old tires, wine bottles, license plates, and pet dogs have all been found in the stomach of a bull shark.

Where it lives
Warm, shallow coastal waters worldwide

What it eats
Fish, other sharks, seals, turtles, birds, other sea animals

Man-eater

The **bull shark** is one of the world's most dangerous sharks. It attacks swimmers and surfers without warning. This shark can live in both salt water and fresh water. It is a danger to people in the ocean as well as in rivers and lakes.

The bull shark lives in shallow water, making it more dangerous to humans.

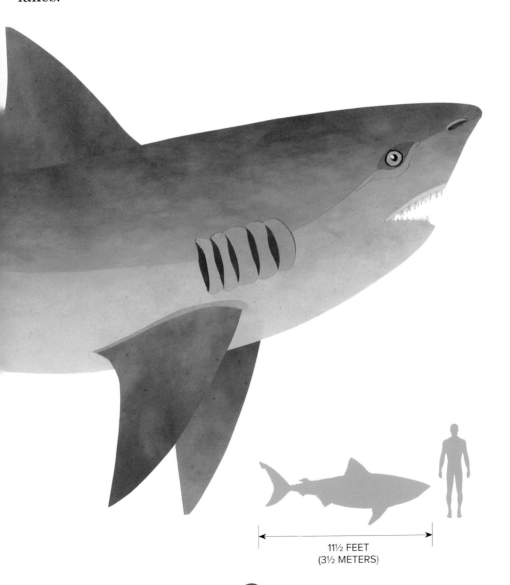

11½ FEET
(3½ METERS)

Surprisingly dangerous

The **hippopotamus** is one of the most dangerous large animals in the world. This huge animal spends most of its time in rivers and lakes. It looks big and slow but it can run as fast as a horse. It may charge if its path to the water is blocked, or if its baby is in danger.

Where it lives
Central and southern Africa

What it eats
Grass, water plants

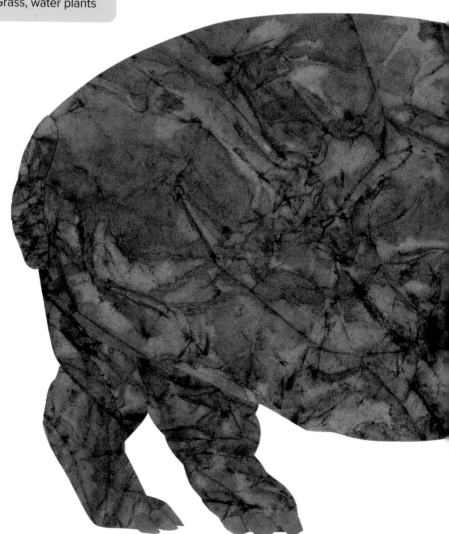

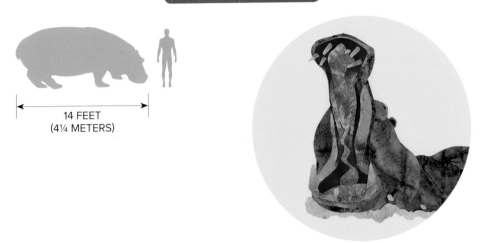

14 FEET
(4¼ METERS)

The hippo defends its territory and its family with a huge mouth and long tusks.

Don't touch me!

The bright colors of the **poison dart frog** tell predators "I'm poisonous— leave me alone." In fact, the skin of one frog contains enough poison to kill an elephant. Native hunters dip their blowgun darts in the frog's poison. These frogs are not dangerous to humans unless they are handled or eaten.

Poison dart frogs acquire their toxins from the insects they eat.

1 INCH
(2½ CENTIMETERS)

Where it lives
Rain forests of Central and South America

What it eats
Insects and worms

Blow-up fish

To protect itself from predators, the **puffer fish** inflates its body like a prickly balloon. Its flesh contains a deadly toxin, but it is harmless to humans unless it is eaten.

In Japan, chefs must have a special license to cook puffer fish. They are careful not to serve the most poisonous parts of the fish.

Where it lives
Atlantic, Pacific, and Indian Oceans

What it eats
Shrimp, shellfish, algae

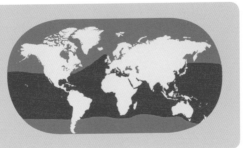

12 INCHES
(30 CENTIMETERS)

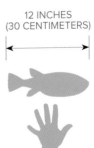

Pretty poison

The **sea snake** is one of the most venomous animals in the world. These reptiles breathe air, but live in the ocean. They do not usually threaten humans. But sea snakes trapped in fishing nets have sometimes fatally bitten people.

Sea snakes are graceful in the water, but they don't move well on land.

3 FEET
(91 CENTIMETERS)

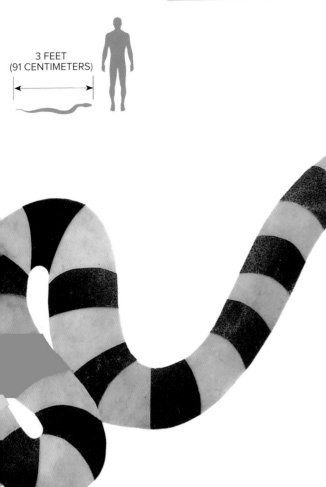

Venomous animals inject their poison with fangs, spines, or stingers.

Poisonous animals must be touched or eaten to be dangerous. Their skin, organs, or other body parts contains poison.

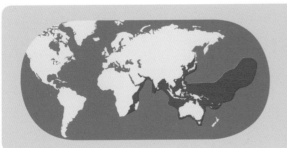

Where it lives
Tropical Pacific and Indian Oceans
What it eats
Fish, squid, octopuses

Giant predator

The **Kodiak bear** and its relative the polar bear are the largest carnivores living on land. A Kodiak bear may attack if it is surprised or if it thinks its cubs are in danger. These bears will sometimes stalk, kill, and eat a human.

10 FEET
(3 METERS)

In the fall, a Kodiak bear prepares to hibernate, or sleep through the winter. It may eat 90 pounds (41 kilograms) of food a day.

Kodiak bears are speedy—they can run as fast as a horse for short distances.

Where it lives
Islands off the south coast of Alaska

What it eats
Deer, small mammals, fish, insects, roots, nuts, berries

Transparent trouble

The delicate **box jellyfish** isn't easy to spot as it drifts through the sea. It doesn't look dangerous, but its venom is some of the most lethal in the animal world. A swimmer stung by its tentacles can die within minutes.

The box jellyfish has 24 eyes arranged around its body, or bell.

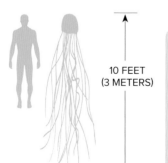

10 FEET
(3 METERS)

Where it lives
The tropical Indian and southwest Pacific Ocean

What it eats
Fish, squid, shrimp

Watch your step.

Anyone wading in the warm waters of the South Pacific Ocean should watch out for the **stonefish.** As it rests on the sea floor, this fish looks like a chunk of colorful coral. The stonefish does not attack humans, but stepping on it would be a serious mistake. The thirteen spines on its back can inject the deadliest venom of any fish. The venom causes intense pain and sometimes death.

Where it lives
The tropical Indian and southwest Pacific Oceans

What it eats
Fish and shrimp

Stonefish can survive being out of the water for up to 24 hours.

15 INCHES
(38 CENTIMETERS)

Scaly, scary, and big

The **king cobra** is the largest venomous snake in the world. It avoids humans when it can, but will strike if it feels threatened. In Asia, king cobras are responsible for hundreds—perhaps thousands—of human deaths every year.

Where it lives
Southeast Asia

What it eats
Other snakes, birds, small animals

The king cobra is the only snake that builds a nest for its eggs.

One king cobra can inject enough venom to kill an elephant.

18 feet
(5½ meters)

Ocean-going predator

The **saltwater crocodile** is the largest reptile in the world. It is also one of the most dangerous. This man-eater has attacked the boats of sailors in the open sea hundreds of miles from land.

The saltwater crocodile is one of the largest predators on earth.

The saltwater crocodile can weigh as much as 1,500 pounds (680 kilograms).

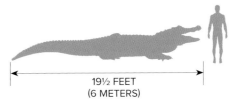

19½ FEET
(6 METERS)

Where it lives
Rivers, lakes, and oceans in Southeast Asia and Australia
What it eats: Fish, shellfish, birds, other reptiles, mammals (including humans)

Banana danger

The **Brazilian wandering spider** is also known as the banana spider. It has the deadliest venom of any spider. It hunts its prey at night, and sleeps in a sheltered place during the day. Sometimes it falls asleep in a bunch of bananas that get picked and shipped to a supermarket. People have been startled to find this large, dangerous spider in their grocery bag.

Where it lives
Northern South America

What it eats
Insects

A bite from this spider can be deadly if a person does not receive medical help.

The Brazilian wandering spider displays its large red jaws when it is threatened.

5½ INCHES
(14 CENTIMETERS)

Deadly spines

The **giant silk moth caterpillar** is a surprisingly dangerous insect. The caterpillar's body bristles with hundreds of tiny spines. If touched, each spine can inject a dose of potent venom. These caterpillars often rest on tree trunks where they are difficult to spot. Accidentally brushing against a giant silk moth caterpillar can be fatal.

Where it lives
Southern Brazil, Argentina, Paraguay, Uruguay

What it eats
leaves

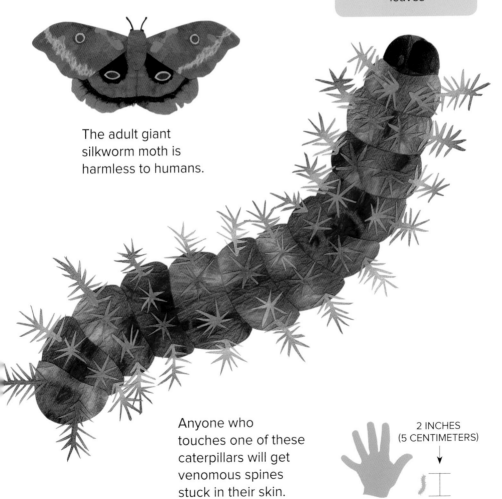

The adult giant silkworm moth is harmless to humans.

Anyone who touches one of these caterpillars will get venomous spines stuck in their skin.

2 INCHES
(5 CENTIMETERS)

Hooves and horns

The **Cape buffalo**, a wild relative of the cow, is an extremely dangerous animal. It has sharp hooves, long horns, and a bad temper. It is quick to defend its territory and its young, and it can charge without warning.

Hundreds of people are attacked and killed by Cape buffaloes each year.

A large Cape buffalo can weigh 2,000 pounds (907 kilograms)—as much as a small car.

5 feet (1½ meters)

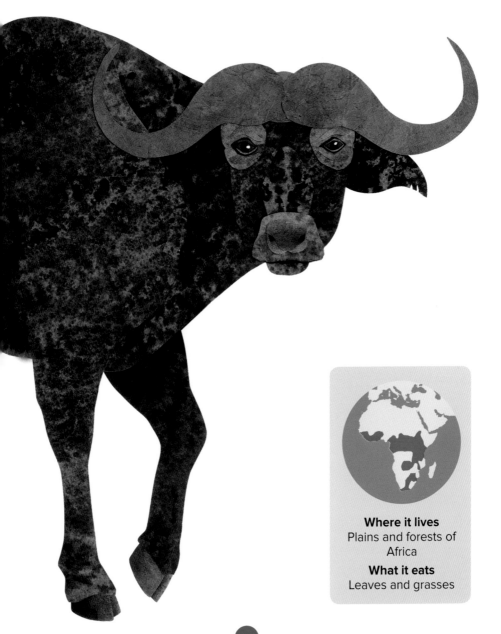

Where it lives
Plains and forests of Africa

What it eats
Leaves and grasses

Colorful warning

The **blue-ringed octopus** is a small, colorful creature. It is found in tide pools along the seashore, where people sometimes pick it up for a closer look. But this harmless-looking creature can be deadly. It has a beak so sharp that its venomous bite often goes unnoticed. A person who handles this little octopus can die in a matter of minutes.

Where it lives
The tropical Indian Ocean and southwest Pacific Ocean

What it eats
Crabs, shrimp, fish

This octopus displays its bright blue rings as a warning when it is frightened.

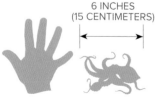

6 INCHES
(15 CENTIMETERS)

One blue-ringed octopus contains enough toxin to kill more than 10 people.

Shocking!

The **electric eel** lives in the murky river waters of South America. It hunts by stunning its prey with a strong jolt of electricity. This eel also defends itself with an electric shock. It can produce a charge that is strong enough to kill a human.

The eel generates a weak electric field to help it find its prey.

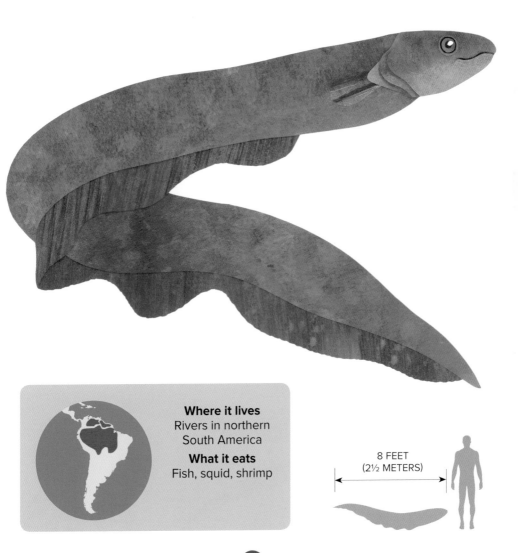

Where it lives
Rivers in northern South America

What it eats
Fish, squid, shrimp

8 FEET
(2½ METERS)

Fearsome lizard

The **Komodo dragon** is the world's largest lizard. It lives on a few islands in the Pacific Ocean. It hunts goats, other large and small animals, and sometimes humans. It also eats dead animals. This huge reptile is an ambush hunter. It hides and waits for its prey to get close. Then it lunges and grabs it.

Where it lives
Komodo Island and a few other Indonesian islands

What it eats
Goats, water buffalo, small animals, other Komodo dragons, humans

A full-grown Komodo dragon can swallow a goat whole.

10 FEET
(3 METERS)

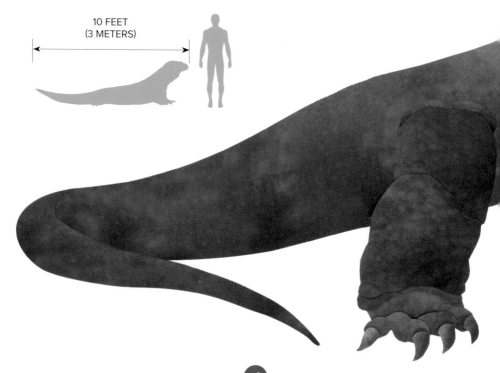

The Komodo dragon has toxic saliva. If its victim escapes after being bitten, the Komodo dragon will follow and wait for its bite to take effect.

Big bird

The **cassowary** is the world's most dangerous bird. This flightless bird lives in dense tropical forests. It is shy and tries to avoid people. But if it feels threatened, it can deliver a deadly kick with its powerful legs.

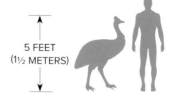

5 FEET
(1½ METERS)

The cassowary has a long, sharp claw on each foot. This claw can slice open a predator—or human—that has gotten too close.

Where it lives
Australia and New Guinea

What it eats
Seeds, leaves, fruit, insects, frogs

Beautiful killer

The **tiger** is the world's largest and most dangerous cat. The tiger's orange coat and black stripes help it hide in the forests and tall grass where it lives. Most tigers hunt deer and other animals. A few become man-eaters, usually because they are old or injured and can't catch wild prey.

Where it lives
India, Southeast Asia, China

What it eats
Deer, buffalo, large and small animals, humans

Tigers are endangered and could become extinct in the wild if they are not protected.

8 FEET
(2½ METERS)

Man's best friend?

Most pet **dogs** are gentle, loving companions. But in some parts of the world there are millions of feral dogs—dogs without owners. These dogs sometimes attack people, and their bites can cause serious injuries. A greater danger is rabies, a deadly disease that is spread by the slightest nip from an infected dog. Rabies kills tens of thousands of people every year.

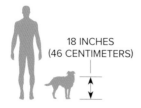

18 INCHES
(46 CENTIMETERS)

Dogs of different breeds vary greatly in size. But most feral dogs are mid-size.

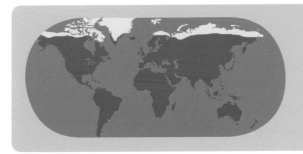

Where it lives
Worldwide, except polar regions

What it eats
Small mammals, frogs, reptiles, garbage

There may be more than 200 million feral dogs in the world.

Deadliest of all

It is probably safe to say that no one likes the **mosquito.** This insect is found almost everywhere on earth. Its bite results in an annoying itch. The mosquito's bite can also transmit deadly illnesses. Every year, more than one million people die from diseases carried by mosquitoes, mostly in tropical countries. This makes it the most dangerous animal of all.

The itching from a mosquito bite is caused by chemicals in the insect's saliva.

Only female mosquitoes have the mouthparts that are used for sucking blood.

H

↑

½ INCH
(1¼ CENTIMETERS)

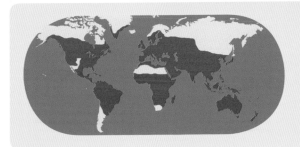

Where it lives
Worldwide, except desert and extreme arctic regions

What it eats
Plant nectar, blood

Mosquitoes lay their eggs on water. Even a bottle cap can hold enough water to hatch a brood of mosquitoes.

How many people are killed by these animals each year?

All of the animals in this book can kill. But some of the deadliest creatures on earth don't actually kill many people. The most dangerous animals are not always the ones we'd expect . . .

	Animal	Human Deaths	More Facts
	bull shark	fewer than 1	Each year, 5–10 people around the world are killed by sharks—mostly white, tiger, and bull sharks.
	hippopotamus	300–500	Hippos are vegetarians, but their huge jaws and tusks can be deadly.
	poison dart frog	no recorded deaths	People that live near this frog know not to handle or eat it.
	puffer fish	3–10	Not everyone knows that this fish is poisonous, and each year a few people die from eating it.
	sea snake	fewer than 1	This snake is shy and tries to avoid people, so sea snake deaths are rare.
	Kodiak bear	fewer than 1	Not many people live where this bear does, so human-bear encounters are rare.
	box jellyfish	100	This jellyfish has killed more than 5,000 people over the past 60 years.
	stonefish	fewer than 1	There are just 5 recorded deaths due to stonefish venom.
	king cobra	1,000	The king cobra tries to avoid people. But its relative the Indian cobra causes tens of thousands of deaths every year.

Animal	Human Deaths	More Facts
saltwater crocodile	15	Other crocodiles kill as many as 1,500 people a year, mostly in Africa and India.
Brazilian wandering spider	fewer than 1	Most people who are bitten survive if they get medical attention.
Giant silk moth caterpillar	2–5	These caterpillars cluster on tree trunks, so victims may have touched several at the same time.
Cape buffalo	250	Human encounters with this bad-tempered, powerful animal often end badly.
blue-ringed octopus	fewer than 1	A total of 13 deaths have been recorded. Probably more deaths were not recognized.
electric eel	fewer than 1	No one really knows. Probably some drowning deaths were due to electrocution by this eel.
Komodo dragon	fewer than 1	Fortunately, these dragons have a small habitat and seldom encounter people.
cassowary	fewer than 1	We know of only 1 or 2 people that have been killed by a cassowary.
tiger	60–100	Most human deaths are the work of just a few tigers that have learned to see humans as food.
dog	55,000	Dog attacks kill people every year. But rabies, a disease spread by dog bite, is much more deadly.
mosquito	1,000,000	The most dangerous animal of all spreads deadly diseases with its bite.

Glossary

carnivore
An animal that eats flesh.

electric field
The region around an electrically charged object. The eel's weak electric field interacts with the electric field produced by all animals, and the eel can sense that another creature is nearby.

electricity
A form of energy that is generated by charged particles.

fatal
Deadly.

feral
A tame or domesticated animal that has gone wild, or that is born wild.

lethal
Deadly, causing death.

man-eater
An animal that kills and eats humans.

poisonous
In the animal world, a creature with poison in its skin or flesh. It must be handled or eaten to cause harm.

predator
An animal that kills and eats other animals.

prey
An animal hunted and eaten by a predator.

tentacle
A long, thin, flexible part of an animal's body. It may be used for moving, grasping something, or delivering a venomous sting.

tide pool
A pool of sea water left on the shore when the ocean goes out at low tide. It is often home to many small sea creatures.

toxin
A poison produced by a living thing.

venom
A poisonous fluid produced by animals as a predatory or defensive weapon.

venomous
In animals, a creature that injects venom with teeth, fangs, spines, or stingers.

Bibliography

Alligators and Crocodiles. By Malcolm Penny. Crescent Books, 1991.

The Animal Book. By Steve Jenkins. Houghton Mifflin, 2013.

Animal Life. By Heidi and Hans Jürgen Koch and Martin Rasper. H. F. Ullmann, 2008.

Dangerous Creatures. By Angela Wiles. Kingfisher, 2003.

Dramatic Displays. By Tim Knight. Heinemann Library, 2003.

Encyclopedia of Reptiles and Insects. Edited by Dr. Glen Shea and Dan Bickel. Fog City Press, 2004.

Extreme Nature. By Mark Caradine. HarperCollins, 2005.

How Animals Work. By David Burnie. DK Publishing, 2010.

Life on Earth. By David Attenborough. Little, Brown and Company, 1979.

Nature's Predators. By Michael Bright, Robin Kerrod, and Barbara Taylor. Anness Publishing, 2003.

The Private Lives of Animals. By Roger Caras. Grosset and Dunlap, 1974.

Reef. By Scubazoo. DK Publishing, 2007.

Smithsonian Super Nature Encyclopedia. By Derek Harvey. DK Publishing, 2012.

Venom. By Steve Backshall. New Holland, 2007.

For Robin

www.hmhco.com

The illustrations in this book were done in torn- and cut-paper collage. The text type was set in Proxima Nova and New Century Schoolbook. The display type was set in Geometric.

ISBN 978-0-544-93808-3 hardcover
ISBN 978-1-328-84170-4 paperback

Manufactured in China
SCP 10 9 8 7 6 5 4 3 2 1
4500661377

LEXILE: 860
F&P: R

40